F

ISLINGTON

Please return this item on or before the last date stamped below or you may be liable to overdue charges. To renew an item call the number below, or access the online catalogue at www.islington.gov.uk/libraries. You will need your library membership number and PIN number.

1/17

TRANS FL 8/18

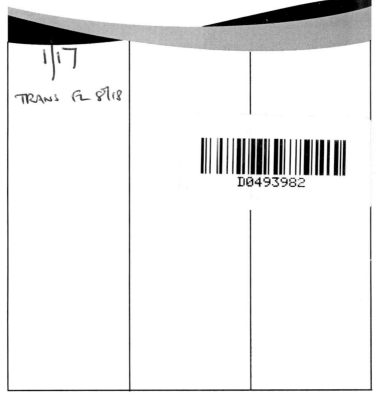

D0493982

Islington Libraries

020 7527 6900   **www.islington.gov.uk/libraries**

SEAN O'BRIEN

Downriver

PICADOR

First published 2001 by Picador
an imprint of Pan Macmillan Limited
Pan Macmillan, 20 New Wharf Road, London N1 9RR
Basingstoke and Oxford
Associated companies throughout the world
www.panmacmillan.com

ISBN 978-0-330-48195-3

9 8 7 6 5 4 3

A CIP catalogue record for this book is available from
the British Library.

Phototypeset by Intype London Ltd
Printed and bound in the UK by
CPI Mackays, Chatham ME5 8TD

Visit **www.picador.com** to read more about all our books and to buy
them. You will also find features, author interviews and news of any author
events, and you can sign up for e-newsletters so that you're always first to hear
about our new releases.

For Douglas and Peter, Peter and Douglas

Contents

Acknowledgements

The Guardian, *The Independent*, *Interchange*, *Kunapipi*, *London Magazine*, *London Review of Books*, *British Council New Writing*, *A Paean for Peter Porter*, *Poetry Ireland Review*, *Poetry Review*, *Poetry Wales*, *Red Herring*, *Recreation*, *Stand*, *Subtext*, *The Sunday Times* and the *Times Literary Supplement*.

A number of these poems appeared in a pamphlet, *The Ideology* (Smith Doorstop, 1997).

'The Genre' was commissioned for the Poetry Society's website under the Poetry Places scheme. 'Last Orders at the Fusilier, Forest Hall' was commissioned by BBC Radio 4 for *A Book of Hours*, broadcast on National Poetry Day, 1999. 'A Northern Assembly' was commissioned by New Writing North for the Northern Cultural Debate at the 1999 Durham Literature Festival. 'Poem for a Psychiatric Conference' was commissioned by the Neuropsychiatric Department of Newcastle Royal Victoria Hospital, and was published in *The Construction of Power and Authority in Psychiatry*, edited by Phil Barker and Chris Stevenson (Butterworth-Heinemann, 2000) and *Beyond Bedlam*, edited by Matthew Sweeney and Ken Smith (Anvil).

The author is grateful to the British Council and the Society of Authors for support in completing this book.

Welcome, Major Poet!

We have sat here in too many poetry readings
Wearing the liberal rictus and cursing our folly,
Watching the lightbulbs die and the curtains rot
And the last flies departing for Scunthorpe.
Forgive us. We know all about you.
Autumn gives way to midwinter once more,
As states collapse, as hemlines rise, as we miss both,
And just as our teeth fall discreetly into our handkerchiefs,
Slowly the bones of our co-tormentees will emerge
Through their skins. QED and *hic jacent*.
Except we are seated bolt upright on customized
'Chairs' of the torturers' school. Here it comes,
Any century now, the dread declaration:
And next I shall read something longer. Please
Rip out our nails and accept your applause!
Stretch-limo back to the Ritz and ring home:
Bore the arse off your nearest and dearest instead,
Supposing they haven't divorced you already
Or selfishly put themselves under a train.
Please call them, at length and at public expense.
Send flunkies for cold Stolichnaya, an ox
Or an acre of coke and a thousand-quid hooker.
Why not make it three, in a chariot
Flown to your penthouse by eunuchs on leopards?
Whatever you like, only spare us the details of when
You were struck by your kinship with Dante and Vergil.
And don't feel obliged to remind us just now
What it was Robert Lowell appeared to be saying –
You'd read him the poem you mean to read us –

When the doors of the lift he was in and you weren't
Began closing. Just leave us the screams
You could hear as the vehicle descended: *Poor Cal.*
Up to then he'd been perfectly normal. Ah, well.

Acheron, Phlegethon, Styx

for Peter Reading

Now they're bricked over and leaking
Victorian adipose into the friable earth
In the heat of a seven-year drought,
They deliver that steady industrial suck-fart
(Like a Scots Pie machine making
Full use of the eyelids and sphincters of pigs)
At the foot of the drainshaft, down in the cack
With rubbers, rags and jaundiced *Telegraph*s
Rolled up in twos, sworn on by plumbers –
Themselves long pulled under –
For checking the flush. Furthermore
The crimson hiss of the exhausted brain,
Its library all clarted pages, corridors
Knee-deep in grease, the gridlocked blood
Attempting pinhole exits at the eyeballs.
Gore and shite, crap-nebulae
And greasy bubbles, steadily hurled
Downstream in a stench of finality. Cheers!

Nineties

Let's drift again in these vast solitudes,
The beer-and-tabs Sargasso of the shore,
Anachronistic legal waterholes
Down foggy chares alleged to have two ends –
We'll make a life's work of an evening out.

Let booths and gantries frame a ruined court
That grants our bores' and lone derangers' pleas
A hearing, though the verdict is the clock's –
Long boxes, six black horses, frosty plumes,
The diggers leaning on their spades to smoke.

Far overhead, a coal train grinds its way
Across the viaduct. A grimy clang
From the cathedral, echoed. Please call home.
Tonight's the nineteenth century *sans* crowds,
A boozers' heaven lit by blue dog-stars

Whose image in the empty river draws
Fanatics to the bridges for dispatch –
Spent gambling men we used to read about,
They seem to wear our faces as they plunge
In sequence from the parapets, as though

To cancel with a gesture thirty years
Drunk dry with infidelity and waste.
They print the water with their leader-dots . . .
Theirs was the truly historical work,
The ground on which we've been arraigned tonight –

Since we've outlived both usefulness and art –
A failure to imagine properly
Our place in the supporting cast, to move
From *rhubarb* to the boneyard in a blink . . .

As if there might be politics afoot,
The night the southside arsenal went up
The people thronged the quays like citizens.
Blood-lit in the inferno of the towns
They hailed their unimportant misery.
The river boiled red-black past walls of flame
And watermen like local Charons cried
Beneath the stairs for passing trade, their arms
Outspread like angels in the burning rain
Of lath and plaster, flesh and cobblestones
That blinded the cathedral weathercocks
And put the heat on whore and judge alike.

Or so the picture shows, that no one sees,
Crammed in beside a turning of the stairs:
Old Testament confusion, modern dress,
And on his non-existent crag, the bard
Who's too far gone to say he told them so.

II

Your hundred streets, your twenty names, all gone.
A stink of burning sofas in the rain,
Of pissed-on mattresses, and poverty's
Spilt milk, its tiny airless rooms designed
To illustrate the nature of subjection
To its subjects. They tell me politics
And history are done: here's grease

Extruded from the dripping tar-skinned walls
Of workingmen's hotels; the ropes of hair
Trapped in the sinks; the names perpetually denied
A hearing, waiting in the smoky halls
For their appointments with an age that bred
And killed and then forgot them – names that now
Forget themselves, the air's mere allegations,
Faces that the mirrors do not hold,
Lockers with no contents, neither razors
Nor the Bible nor an envelope of dimps
Preserved against the certainty of worse.
So Billy, Tommy, Jackie – did you live?
Could it be you that Benjamin's
Averted angel is ignoring now
As once again you leave your flooded graves
Like newsreel ghosts to greet the Kaiser's guns?

III

Blind walls and hidden roadways running down
To water. Black windows wedged with newsprint,
Morning after morning of the afterlife,
Anacoluthon of streets and bars.
                    The bar as survival, as figment,
Dog on the shelf and women to rights,
The Hole in the Corner where dead men meet,

The dead of emphysema
And of pneumoconiosis,
                    bickering
Beyond the grave like kids.

There is football, or football. Occasional boxing:
Jimmy Wilde and Woodcock, Billy Hardy

Brave as owt
and carefully done down,
A lesson you have to pretend you've forgotten.

Or else there was Hitler, that flag-waving cunt.
Should have been a referee. Should have been hung
By the balls and then shot at. The Jarmans want tellt.

*

Eternity's offside; a lockout.
It's stilted black coal-staithes becoming aesthetics.

It's the exacerbated calm,
The grey summer nights at the end of the world

Through which an old bloke walks his dog
Across that shitty stretch of no man's grass

Because it's his vocation,
Middle distant citizen of patience.

The Ideology

for John Hartley Williams

When the poem sneaks up on itself –
It wishes to be intimate
With history – it finds itself leaning
From a footbridge on the cutting,

Round at the back of the district
In part of the never-was Umpties
Where somebody probably dreamed of a cinema
Out on this far edge of town, that could show

Fort Apache for ever. And this is what's
Never been noticed or built on.
The clinkered slopes are foxed with autumn.
A lot to take in, even here. The desire

To pause, to repose, like a white-trash Horatian
Instructed in death as in what comes before it –
Descent through the fiery circles of drink
And finance, with a box from the Co-op to finish.

Instead, then, the poem imagines
The smell and the oil after coal-smoke
Here in the after-tea quiet
With nights drawing in for back-end,

And strangers' leaves arriving on the lawn
And people remarking on this
Before switching their fires on. Instead, then,
The gaze of the red lamp resembles

The rowan trees' troubling berries.
Site of pagan industry, the poem thinks –

Or Nature and Industry,
Weed coiling over the tracks,

Sliding the slates from the lineside hut
Until willowherb stands in the doorway,
Obsolete, proprietorial
And cap in hand. No woolly peach in view.

The sound that hangs behind the air
Could be wind off the hills or the one train a day
Hauling coal from the strip-mine.
Do you believe? believe truly? the poem enquires

In the soft, educational voice
That means, Not any more, not entirely.
From westward the white sky comes over on rollers
And up the hill on a far estate

A bus is masking one by one the lamps
As they harden from pink towards orange.
What cannot be said, the poem thinks,
Is the necessity in it, that means

A gang of girls is out in this.
Beneath a streetlamp by the pub
They stand with folded arms, comparing clothes,
Shouting as if they're expecting an echo.

The poem ages them. They go indoors.
They marry or not and bear children
And die, and are found in mid-shriek
In a different poem, still there in the cold

Wearing hardly a stitch, being happy
The way those who live with industrial parks and asbestos
Are happy, because if they weren't they would die,
On the need-to-know basis of beauty and truth.

At the Gate

This is the open gate to summer, beckoning
From the lane's end, at its back
The sound of distant water like applause
From re-grown woods, where sycamores
Have privatized the smoke-skinned chimneystacks.
Gate of summer. Summer of poverty,
Ignorance and Methodism, iron-willed
Pharaonic stone-walled engineering
Waged along vertical valley-sides. Summer
With the coiners hanged, with funeral lace,
With shoddy, mungo, bloody-bibbed
Consumptives carted to the pit.
Vernacular water is having
Its ignorant say, blathering perpetually
Through loopholes in the statute book
And sliding underneath death's door:
So now, as spring accelerates
Across the threshhold into June,
Applause, and then a shock of shame
At all that's irremediably done.

The Eavesdroppers

There are no trains this afternoon.
Nothing is coming
From under the second-hand bathwater sky,
Through the zinc-tasting air,
Over the low hum of half-expectation
That hangs at knee-height where the tracks run away
Past frosty docks and groundsel
At the unadopted edges of allotments.
The clocks have shut down.
Deep in the roofing-felt shanties,
Sputtering quietly next to the kettles
The old gadgees' transistors explain
That the racing's abandoned
And this is our chance 'to enjoy once again
The remarkable day in 1957 when England' *click* –
No trains. But this end of the city
Is lending an ear – 'housewives and the unemployed',
The idle student eking out his blow,
The mortician's receptionist
Bent to her Angela Carter
(A slow day for death), and me doing this.
Never think nobody cares
For that thundery corridor
Painting its Forth into Scotland and back,
For the drizzly grind of the coal-train
Or even the Metro, that amateur transport,
Sparking and chattering every verse-end.
Where and for that matter who
Can we be without them and the world

They continually carry away,
To which, now it's silent, we find
We have spent our lives listening?

Last Orders at the Fusilier, Forest Hall

for Maureen and Eileen

Here's winter now – the first frost on the field,
Black stratocirrus, then a grid of stars
Pinned up behind the roofs. The freezing Bear
Extends a paw across the skies to greet
The North as we roll round: *so put it there*,
The Night Shift say, careerists of the bars.
We strive, we seek, we never bloody yield,
And Peter Beardsley grew up down the street.

So Stuart, Tommy, Micky, Dicky, Ron,
This is the life, with one eye on the clocks,
From boy to gadgee round the Fusilier!

That's ten to. That's another evening gone,
The bar staff crouched like sprinters in the blocks:
Now Letsby Avenue! Time on your beer!

Ravilious

Beneath the great white horse's one green eye,
The goods-train steams in blue-black miniature
Away from us, into the cross-hatched fields.
Perhaps this will be England finally
And not a further painful episode
In the discreet narration of a love
That when it learns its name will have to die.

*

Where are we now? Not on the O.S. sheet.
The wrong side of the glass, we stop to watch
The dapper engine cross a bridge by night
Beside a fingerpost with four ways back
To England, closed to us. We know the place.

*

The next time round, we take the train to see
The watchers down the line, preoccupied
With maps and catalogues, white horses, us.
They close their faces as we pass, to learn
More clearly where they stand and what it means.
At which we guess. All our excursions run
Not to our love but where we lived and died.

Piers Powerbook's Prologue

The conference season that year   was a scorcher,
But I wore Armani   befitting the ambience,
Being both journo   and sensual man,
And went down to the world   to catch the day's wonders,
To clock the main marvels   and so-called enigmas.

That sweating September   beside Blackpool seafront
I felt a bit sleepy,   a smidgen hungover
And somewhat estranged   by the night before's Es,
So by the Ramada's   mezzanine fountain
I dozed like a toad   in a hatbox instead.

The dream I dreamed there   was a digitized triumph:
The virtual arse-end   of England, a field
Of old sidings and willowherb,   slathered in junk mail.
Above, a great tower   that inked out the sun
With its finger, as meanwhile   its residents sang

Like canary-cum-corvines   aloft in their carrion column.
Beneath sank a festering pit   like a privatized nick
Or a carpark, or both   with community care
A remote aspiration   and here in the meantime
The creatures of mad   with the citizens' charter

Crammed in the puss   to prevent them
From biting their tongues off –   not that they talk much.
Between, on the interface,   seemed to be grazing
The mere pixelled public   across the broad precinct,
Fondly supposing whatever affairs   of the pocket

And heart they pursued   were their own.
While the hewers of hamburgers   sweated their kecks off
On minimum wage   to fuel the fantasy
The tough were out shopping   parading like tarts
In Vivien Westwood   in Engels and Spencer,

Umbrellas aloft   in the patter of homilies
Aimed at their head   by the chattering class,
By the palace of Lambeth   *The Catholic Herald*
Your soaraway *Sun* and *Hello!*   and Ms Melanie Philips.
And meanwhile the business   got down to the business

Of selling us back to ourselves –   in a summery soundtrack,
The samples of samples   of retro-*nuevo* classics –
This England, this island   of any-old-irony.
You won't be surprised   if I tell you it gave me
A bone, a banana,   a right Baudrill[h]ard[on],

This forest of symbols   with no firm foundation.
There for the taking,   the dead centre ground
Of the national being   was blown all to buggery,
Loaned out to landfill   and lickspittle speech,
Plus the lame and the halt   like a Biblical epic.

It lacked Charlton Heston.   It lacked a high concept.
It needed a niche   and a non-union shop.
Then up sprang a wight,   boss-eyed like a wanker,
A priest and his lady,   a lawyer as well
And all their bambinos   (precocious in oratory).

His name was a blur   like the far-off oasis
You know's a mirage   but are trying to reach . . .
By Christ, they were moral.   They never inhaled.
They were prone to mere error   and rather like us
Except with more money   (OK to hang on to, OK?)

Though most of us haven't   a court to our names
Or a Hartlepool monkey   from Hell, who can caper
And whisper as well   as a weasel, a Waldegrave,
A wight-wing fanatic   disguised as a don
Until you can't tell   which is arse, which is elbow

And seem to believe   between money and morals
A fissure is driven   whose function's to prove
We can learn to behave   and it won't cost a penny.
The poor will be good   and the rich will be safe
If we'd all just be straight,   if we'd all just get married –

Let's carry on shopping   and shagging the kids
As we did in the Fifties, except   it's in colour, on cable.
Empirical England!   Install it today! . . .
Well, pass me the sickbag,   I said when I woke
All alone by the fountain.   But soon I was sorely afraid:

Had I missed the main feature?   I legged it like Linford
Straight down to the Gardens   and barely got in.
I was one rung from leprosy   late, at the back,
And the service was already   well under way.
There was speaking in tongues,   there were knee-jerk reactions,

And heretics sat on their hands   and the text
Was a war of some sort   which the faithful would win
Against doubt and division   and organized labour.
When up sprang a wight,   boss-eyed like a wanker,
A priest and his lady,   a lawyer as well.

Are you all sitting ducks? he enquired.   *Well, then I'll begin.*
Woah, I said, *woah,   now hang on a minute,*
Woe to the country   whose king is a child
But the minders were on me   and putting me out.
I woke in a heap in the carpark   with Nicholas Scott.

You've caught the wrong conference,   *Nick*, I remarked.
Are you sure? he said,   hailing a policeman.
Woe to the country whose king   is a child.
Vanity. Vanity. All of it. Vanity.

A Northern Assembly

So, then, let's strike a northern light
To blind those armies of the night
Who always place a southern spin
Around the state we're living in.

Remove the Westminster diktat?
Who wouldn't go along with that?
But can your North be North like mine?
Who gets to draw the borderline?

Who says where North begins and ends?
Are Makems and Smogmonsters friends?
Are Monkeyhangers on the run
Since Mandy's flit to Islington?

And what about the Boro? Soft:
I hear the clank of Chairman Croft.
And what about, you know, Gateshead,
Whose rusty Angel guards the shed

Where only thirty cared enough
To come and hear you do your stuff?
If folks don't think there's much at stake
For Pity Me and Bolam Lake,

And use their Saturdays to shop,
Not give big government the chop,
What chance of making Tory Blair
Firstly: listen, second: care?

– For in the mind of Chairman Tone
Democracy means Tone alone
Deciding what we all love best
While Warden Straw bangs up the rest.

New Labour likes to share its bed
With those who want the unions dead
And sent in Dr Cunningham
To make us love Monsanto spam–

Bizarre: one half school-dinner-hag,
The other Dracula in drag,
Living proof that food mutation
Raises you above your station.

Pols of this stripe don't rely
On principle to get them by:
If they cannot slag they bore.
Persistence: nine parts of the law.

When no one can be arsed to cast
A Eurovote, perhaps the last
Thing the electorate requires
Is mini-Quins and Browns and Byers

Crowding to the public trough:
The pols have pissed the people off
By playing at democracy
While flying to the moon for free.

So, world and politics on fire,
The poet chooses to retire
Where the pastoral is found,
In Tyneside's secret pleasure ground

Come North by North to Forest Hall,
Most South American of all
The suburbs where the pits were sunk.
Here giant snakes pursue the drunk

Administrators of the arts
In stolen Kular's shopping carts.
Here Spanish is the loving tongue,
Like music from the iron lung

Of pitmen sacked and pensioned off
To man the lunchtime bars and cough,
While on the news a sycophant
Extols the, well, the Siemens plant.

What is true North, what's bogus South?
Insert your money in your mouth
To prove your aim's as serious
As mere prosaic theory is:

A North that's not a party game
But can support a sovereign claim
Begins at Humberside and knows
How Andrew Marvell's metre goes –

Let North, from Humber's shore to Tweed
Exist in verse, if not yet deed,
And let a poem legislate
For this ideal imagined state,

The theoretical address
No king has managed to suppress.
Spirits of water, coal and stone –
Pick up the Muse's telephone

And let us hear your Northernness.
Affirm, affirm: this North says yes.
Let's say that we'll not now endure
The treatment suited to manure –

Let's aim to chuck a few lumps back:
Now then Cockneys, eat this cack.
From Cockermouth to Withernsea,
The North – the North is poetry.

It means that we can't tolerate
The dim, the daft, the second-rate –
In poetry or politics –
This is the North and not the sticks –

Still less expect the working class
To keep electing one more crass
Machine-head from the civic hall
To keep on taking home his ball.

So, bent old cooncillors, play dead
Or end up in the nick instead;
Prods and Masons, racists, Papes,
Wash your hands and wipe your tapes.

The latest crowd of suits won't do
To state what's beautiful and true:
If North is North and South is Wrong
The fact deserves a decent song,

Not subliterate conference papers
Scrawled by would-be history-shapers.
By all means rouse the Meadowell
But also learn to bloody spell.

But what the Northern sceptic fears
Is what mysteriously appears
In every meeting-place: the rump
Excreted from the parish pump,

A stale, unappetizing bunch –
The thick, the bought, the out to lunch,
Carnivores in eco-hats
Empire-builders, toadies, twats:

The shite that rises to the top
But couldn't run a corner shop
Somehow contrives to represent
Itself as fit for government . . .

You wear that visionary stare,
Believing that you're almost there.
You must have nothing else to do.
You must think we're as daft as you.

As Eliot said – you may recall –
No, that's not what we meant at all.
We want our representatives urbane,
Equipped with fully working brain,

Not furnished with opinions from
The P.M.'s spokesman's CD-rom.
In fact the North's not paradise.
Let's not indulge its favourite vice

– The sentimental one-eyed view
Of what's well known to me and you,
The 'natural nobility'
That whinges to be let in free

But can't be arsed to learn its trade
And sing whatever is well-made.
I'm told you shouldn't take the Mick
Because the North can't stand the stick –

To which the modern poet replies
That what she loves she'll satirize,
While those who cannot take a joke
Find reasons to be shooting folk:

Milosevic and Jean Le Pen
Began somewhere, as local men.

Baltica

for Laura Rota i Roca and Jens Fabrin

The pages of water are always revising themselves,
As if the truth is out there somewhere
In the blue contested space that giant ferries cross
Like diplomats, with huge discretion.

Land stops and begins with three dots . . .
Where we wait on a finger of concrete,
With buffers and warnings and grey wooden pilings
A vessel has lately bashed into.

This is the kind of a town
There must be where a ferry departs,
Somewhere the rails can run through,
Where no one lives and everybody comes from –

Bars, bad girls, a brand of Schnapps.
At six o'clock it closes down
And drinks itself to death,
Surfacing cross-eyed and swearing on bicycles.

Meanwhile a dredger is roaring away
To preserve the deep channel –
A frightening hungover military noise
Which has only volume to lend the debate

Over whether in fact we shall manage
To travel, or ought to go back where we started.
We sit on the bollards in sunshine, with crosswords
Like treasure-maps, dreaming our turn

To set out from one rock to the next.
Twenty feet down the green inshore Baltic
Sways gently, its spread hands commending
A breathable otherworld,

Names we cannot yet pronounce,
Glottal-stopped landfalls, ship-drinking gulfs
To be glugged with the brine
From a tin of sunk herring. Plenitude

Of copper coin, receipts and destinations!
Enviable archipelagians! Give us
A go on your rusty red coasters
Crammed with foot-passengers,

All staring ceremonially east.
Hold tight to your ruinous trawlers, raucous
With caterwaul Danish-and-Western.
For what could be simpler than loving the distance –

The numberless low-lying needlepoint islands
That narrow to barely believable farms,
The peaceable saltire, a stony beach
With firs and two swans, where a ferry sets out?

Riding on the City of New Orleans

From the Crescent City slowly
Over stormy Pontchartrain,
Through Louisiana dusk
And into Mississippi night,
To Tennessee and Illinois,
Which are impossible,
From rémoulade and sin towards
A klieg-lit German paradise,
The train goes, crying *Train, Train.*
We are travelling so slowly,
Two-four on the joints, two-four,
The journey could be proof, almost,
That home, or hope, or what you need
Are only now departing: run
And you could board it still
Beneath the cover of that cry.
That voice is returned from the walls
Of graves in the permanent lockdowns,
Over sweating antebellum lawns
Beneath the levee. Or it stirs
In a snaredrum sat tight in its kit
On the stage of the Wild Kingdom Bar,
A concrete expression of popular will
Where music and murder take place
Every night of the long week of Sundays.
Train, the voice whispers:
Its breath clouds a saxophone's bell.
Train, down the tarpaper length
Of a shotgun slavehouse

Still upright beside the reactor. *Train*,
And the poor are once more reinvented,
Sleeping in the slowly rocking coach.
To name the states that lie
On either hand from sea to sea
Is neither here nor there, and to dismount
At the edge of a field, or a road, or a river
And watch the train depart, becoming
Swaying lights and then the dark
In which its very name recedes,
Could make a man forget his own
Or stay repeating it forever.

Indian Summer

these iron comforts, reasonable taboos
JOHN ASHBERY

Look at this frosty red rose leaning over
The milk on the step. Please take it. But leave me
Its fragrance, its ice in the mind, to remember you by.
The girlfriends of afternoon drinkers
(O *the criminal classes, their bottle-tanned lasses*)
Have locked up their halters and shorts –
Being practical girls, they have understood soon
What I struggle with late, getting grit in my eyes –
That the piss-palace garden is windy and dim
When the heat goes at four. It is over again.
Now the engineer turns up to service the heating
And says: *I see your bell's still bust*
From the Charon-cold depths of his anorak hood.
The dark house is a coffin of laws; early closing.
But if the clocks must forever go back
To the meantime of Pluto, leave me your voice,
Its rumour at the confluence of Portugal and Spain,
From whose entwining waters rises, like a shell
Within the echo in the ear, your own supreme Creole.
If I am doomed to winter on the Campo Mediocrita
Whose high plateau becomes the windy shore
Of an ocean with only one side, to wait
Where the howling sunshine does not warm me,
Let me speak your tongue, at least –
For yours is the music the panther laments in,

Retreating to Burradon, yours is the silvery
Script of the spider at midnight,
Your diary is scandal's pleasure-ground
From which a bare instant of cleavage or leg
Is all I shall have to sustain me. And yours
Are the text and the age I should like to be acting:
You lie on the bed of the lawn, painted gold,
With the base of your spine left naked to breathe,
And now I might seal the extravagant promise
To kiss you to life with your name, if for once
You could look at me – do it now – straight
In the eye, without smiling or shaking your head.

Kanji
for G.

Wish you were here, though I never arrived.
Here is a poem with no way in.
There are so many kanji. Each is a gate
Whose key waits on its other side.
The white-gloved taxi-driver keeps one
Safe indoors in the ignition of his linen-covered

Primly pornographic back-seat parlour,
While the bar hostess secretes hers
God knows where about her tiny person.
Professor N. will show me his,
Which could, he says regretfully –
Here's where he stops quoting Shakespeare –

Be mine if I were not, ahem, *gaijin*.
I wonder when the poem might begin.
In restaurants where demons brandish choppers
Crabs the size of manhole covers
Gesture at its shape from holding tanks
As if like the Houdinis of the id

At any moment they'll be free to chase
Half-naked girls down streets of science fiction.
Even to be drunk's a foreign language here:
An empty space to fill in with the hands.
I meet you like a beggar at the airport.
Later, sealed for minutes in a lift,

I brush your dress. Is that your stocking-top,
A clue? I wonder what it might unlock,
Then whether, if I tried, your voice,
Familiar as my own, but infinitely sweeter,
Would suddenly be foreign with regret
And muffled by the closing of the door.

The Grammar School Ghost

Charlotte Square, Newcastle upon Tyne, 1860

The globe was spinning when I left the room,
But it was more than Geography I missed.
First I was impudent. Next I was dead.
You will wait in the corridor. You, boy –
Muddleheaded, dirty-minded, you, boy –

Wait and be struck by Victorian lightning
Aimed by God Almighty down the chimney
In a theorem of fire. QED.
And to this day I wait for Kingdom Come
Within this draughty whitewashed box,

While all the world rewrites itself, while ink
And chalk and sweat and cabbage are displaced
By ozone from the lights, and *Opium*
My secretary dabs between her breasts.
Behind the cloakroom mirror now, I blow

A kiss into her mouth, that lipstick rose
It seems to be her life's work to perfect.
My looks will never touch her, but I'm true,
Admiring the future from afar.
By night I try to love the elements:

Repaired, repaired, then broken yet again,
For years on end the skylight lets me read
The hand of stars that I've been dealt, or watch
The moon ascend behind its pane of ice,
The snow come falling through my empty head.

Cities

and still some down to go
KEN SMITH

What are cities made of? Steam vents. Blue light. Murder.
Steps going down from the dark to the dark
Past yellow helmets aiming anxious lamps, past padded coats
Making sorrowing bearlike gestures of general
But hopelessly inarticulate love, past men
And their haircuts, their eyebeams, unspoken advice.
Everyone knows. Whoever it is must already be dead.
Eviscerated, eyeless, boiled – in a thousand conditions
They wait to be found and lamented, chained
Amid the perpetrator's stinking hoard of symbols:
Nail-clippings, fingerbones, rat hair, milk,
Scorched pages of an ancient book
That holds the key. But down you go
And the hours stretch, and the clocks in the offices
Stare at each other in rigid hysteria.
Your colleagues in the daylight world
Yawn with despair, an hour from sailboats and beer.
But you go on descending until you have left
The last outpost of order some far landing back
Before cast-iron stairs gave way to wood.
Isn't it tempting to dump the aluminium suitcase
And stop here, making a place of this nowhere?
The staircase folds back on itself
And the silent tunnel plunges further in
Under the last of the railbeds, the last bottled river,

Graveyard of oystermen, library of masons, latrine of the
  founders,
Stained-glass temple of carnivorous Morlocks,
Deadlight, corridor, cupboard, box.
Sit with your torch playing over the brickwork
Still hoarse with graffiti – '*looks like Aramaic*' – and listen
To the silence breathing *This is and this is and this is*,
Endlessly folding and reading itself,
A great book made of burlap and dust,
That is simply digesting the world –
Its drips and rustles, the screams from old cases,
Trains that were heading elsewhere
In a previous century. Soon
You will come to believe you have eaten this book,
That your gullet is lined like a tenement room with its print,
That your tongue has illustrations
And your breath must smell of pulp.
Isn't it tempting to answer, *Just give me the reason
And then we'll go up to the air* – it is dawn above ground
And the manholes stand open, steaming
For the resurrection, straight up in the blue
Where we seek reassurance – *go up there
And start to forget it all over again.*

The Underwater Songbook

Songs from the Drowned Book

I

In the beginning was all underwater,
The down-there-not-talked-about time,
Deep North its drowned masonic book
And inaudible bubbles of speech,

Creation a diving-bell seeking its level
Down stone under stone, the slick passages
Fronded by greenery, flashlit by ore
And acetylene candles –

The blind fishes' luminous ballroom,
The pillars of coal, the salt adits, the lead oubliette of the core
And the doors upon doors, all lost
To the surface long since, with the language. Now
Is there anything there, underneath? Is there more?

II

See
I can remember when
All this was manuscript:

How
Down the green deep we tipped
Law-clerks schoolmen state and church

And with them kingliness,
The night we sank the crown
Off Holderness.

Adam delved
And Dives swam
And sank, swam
And sank:
So who was then the gentle man?
Ourselves, or them
Whose deaths we drank?

III

Name me a river.
I'll name you a king.
Then we shall drown him
And his God-given ring.
Drown him in Gaunless,
Drown him in Wear,
Drown him like Clarence,
Except we'll use beer.

Name me a river.
I'll name you a price.
River's not selling –
Take river's advice:
Dead if you cross me,
I'll not tell you twice.

My river's from heaven.
Your river's been sold,
And your salmon have died
Drinking silver and gold.

Your river's a sewer,
A black ditch, a grave,
And heaven won't lend you
The price of a shave.

IV (*Baucis and Philemon in Longbenton*)

– Hinny, mek wor a stotty cake,
Wor needs it for wor bait.
– Hadaway, pet, away and shite:
You'll have to fookin wait.
Or mek yer stotty cake yerself
If yer sae fookin smart.
– Aye, ah will, wor divvent need ye,
Ya miserable tart.

V (*From the Dive Bar of the Waterhouse*)

I was dreaming underwater
When you swam into my bed:
How like you this? The tail, I mean,
And my long hair, rich and red?
A naiad of the standing pools
Of England's locked back yard,
It is because of you, my dear,
That makars live so hard.

Sherry from Kular's (see beggars; see choose)
Red Biddy, Thunderbird, non-booze booze,
Hair oil, Harpic, shit in your shoes –
It's casual drinking, it's paying your dues.

What would you give to know my name
And speak it in your verse,

It's true I loved my iron man
From the depths of his iron bed.
I loved him and my life ran out
And I was left for dead.

I learned how his poem continued
On the far side of the page –
The hero could never distinguish
Tenderness from rage,

And locked me in the iron bed
From dawn till dead of night,
Darning children's jerseys
While my coal-black hair ran white.

I gave him thirteen children
And ten were dead at birth–
Professor now you tell me how
To estimate my worth.

It's true I loved my iron man
From the depths of his iron bed.
I loved him and my life ran out
And I was left for dead.

III LAMENT

Lay the cold boys in the earth
At Mons and Hartlepool:
Prove to anyone who doubts
That blood and iron rule.

Let the river thickly speak
In tongues of silt and lead.
Teach us our impediment:
We cannot face the dead.

Run the waters furnace-red,
Afire all night long.
If we're to live then we've to make
An elemental song:

The object of the exercise
Is furnishing the world
With battleships, and thunderbolts
The gods would once have hurled.

How shall we know ourselves except
As sparks on blood-red streams,
Where fire-tongued our utterance
Incinerates our dreams?

Lay the cold boys in the earth
At Loos and Stockton town.
Still the blazing rivermouth
And shut the engines down.

Bells of lamentation preach
The law from every spire
To those whom nature could not teach
The language of its fire.

Lay the cold boys in the earth
At Passchendaele and Yarm.
Let the headstones hold them safe
From history and harm.

Twenty thousand men ablaze
Have found their lives outrun
As certainly as if you'd killed them
Singly with a gun.

When the tide is singing
At the steel doors of the bay,
Maybe you can catch its drift:
The world has gone away.

O when the tide is singing
At the steel doors of the bay,
Maybe you can catch its drift:
The world has gone away.

Songs from *Downriver*

I ON A BLUE GUITAR (Lulu Banks)

Dreamed I sat on Daddy's knee
By the dirty riverside
He played his blue guitar
I sat and sang and couldn't tell you
If I lived or if I died

Daddy show me how it goes
The dance the devils do in hell
When you play your blue guitar
It seems you do it very well
Live or die I cannot tell

Dreamed my mammy told me once
Life's a prison, not a pleasure
Dreamed my mammy told me once
Good girls never spend their treasure
That was after the event
I thought my treasure wisely spent

II HORIZONTAL (Bobby Smart)

I was never strong on navigation
I could hardly find my way around
I could never see the slightest difference
Between the China Sea and Puget Sound
But I kept my weather eye on the horizon
Certain that wherever I might stray
There's one test I could beat the other guys on
Where there's a broad involved I know my way

Oh, the adjective deriving from horizon
Goodness me
Would that be
Horizontal?
It may take years to reach you
But stay there on the beach
And you will see
If you remain
Horizontal
That neither hurricane, dead calm
Nor an octopus alarm
Nor the fearsome Hellespont'll
Keep me from the place I have to be
Whether what I really want'll
Happen, who can tell
But you'd look lovely horizontal to me

Some people praise the sextant and the compass
And other great devices of the deep
But standing there just marking off the headings
Is guaranteed to send me off to sleep
Of course my seamanship requires refining
But out there where the ocean meets the sky

I know that a young lady is reclining
Just waiting for when I come sailing by

Your mother keeps a rolling pin to warn off
Me and other monsters of the billows
But I recall my clothing was all torn off
When last we laid our heads upon her pillows
The likes of me sustain a great tradition
We draw the straightest line across the sea
So help me by assuming the position
And opening your compasses for me

III SMOKE SIGNALS (Bobby Smart and Sailor Chorus)

Duke Ellington was very firm upon it
Don't smoke stuff unless there's writing on it
But speaking as a fiend whose mind is blown
I generally prefer to roll my own
It's frowned upon by moralists and vicars
The sort who can't get girls to drop their knickers
But I've found the way to win a girl's affection
Is by offering her the use of your . . . connection

Some like em small and some prefer em jumbo
And Doctor John dips his into his gumbo
A spliff made all the difference to Rimbaud
Verlaine took his with arms like this – akimbo –
Mandela liked a drag and so did Tambo
Folks smoke the stuff from Amazon to Humbo
It will endow the straightest whitest combo
With unsuspected talents for the mambo

So come into my lair and be enslaved
Below decks we're remarkably depraved

There's a snap of Rita Hayworth on the wall
And one of Lollobrigida
That could inflame a Frigidaire
In which she's hardly wearing clothes at all

It's a place of unimaginable sin
So convent girls are queuing to get in
And our revels are just itching to beguine
Leave your morals at the door
You won't need them any more
And be sure to tell your sisters where you've been

This is where we all go up in smoke
It's lovely gear – I scored it from a bloke
Who told me that it's Himalayan Black
The Yeti's very favourite type of tack
I couldn't give a knack
If it's pickled monkey-cack
As long as it can pack a proper wack

So sod the Queen and sod your hearts of oak
To sex and drugs I dedicate this toke
– And to music, but not country and not folk
Admit it, I'm a really handsome bloke
I'm Dracula without the opera cloak
And I'm prepared to offer you a poke
But first of all let's have another smoke

IV I DREAM THE RIVER (Susie Rivers)

When I lie down at night I dream the river
It sounds just like the roar of my own blood
I realize that I'll be here for ever
The water is my only neighbourhood

Dreamed of river's work and river's pleasure
Dreamed of pirate queens and men of war
Blood and bones and love and buried treasure
There's nothing but the river any more

Write his name in blood and dirty water –
What remained of that through thick and thin?
The wise girl knows what all the tides have taught her –
The river is the world she's living in

I live there as it roars between the bridges
And when the tide lays bare the stinking mud
The life worth living lingers at its edges
And sometimes it's as if I've understood

How wide the river reaches and how deep
And what it is to be the water's lover
But this is knowledge I can never keep
And soon that river-music makes me sleep
As one day it will take me down for ever

V TIME ON YOUR BEER NOW (The Company)

It's time now let's have your beer
It's time in the Fall and the Golden Ball
Time you were out of here
Time in the Letsby Avenue now
Time in the Dying Gaul
On Scotswood Road and Percy Street
Let time go by the Wall
It's time, my dear, in the Do Feel Queer
There's no time left at all

Time after time in the Paradigm
Time in the Watch This Space
It means it's time when them bells chime
I'm sick of your fuckin face
Time in the Berkeley, time in the Hume
Time in the Leibnitz too
Time in the Baruch Spinoza
And time in the Kants Like You

In Tunis Street, in Tunis Street
It's time in the Blue Manatee
It's time, it's time, it's time on your beer
In the White Man's Grave
In the Price of a Shave
In the Bugger off Back to Sea

It's time in the Clock and the Dog Watch
It's time in the Graveyard Shift
It's time in the Manifesto
(Three times last night police were called
To an ideological rift)
Time in the Pay You Tuesday
Time in the Christ Now What
And time in the Well Then? and well past time
In the Honest I Forgot

The river-bell rings
When the tide roars back
Under the bridges, down in the cack –
Wallsend and Jarrow
The Old Straight and Narrow
Their hollow mouths howling
Time on your beer now. Go back to sea now.
The coppers'll come with a barrow.

O put on your pants and roll off the bed
There's a taxi at the door.
Stop off at the Tomb and the Hanged Man's Head
'Cos you won't be back no more
You're barred, you're barred, as Enid said
With her brush up the crack of your arse
You're barred from the Johns and the Bear and the Queens
But the Cathouse is different class

Leave the meter ticking over
The driver asleep in his cab
You never can tell just what you'll catch
When you drink with a lass in the Crab
Pissed in the Gents
And the Landlord's Bent
Spark out in the Night Was Young
Brayed in the Privates
Frenched in the Pope
Then you fell off the Bottom Rung
You measured the Coffin
You counted the Bricks
And awoke in the Iron Lung
Time on yer beer
Time on yer beer
Time on yer beer now PLEASE!

Sports Pages

1 Proem

From ancient days until some time last week
Among the poet's tasks was prophecy.
It was assumed the language ought to speak
The truth about a world we've yet to see;
Then in return for offering this unique
And eerie service, poets got their fee:
And yet, what any poem has to say's
Bound up with all the vanished yesterdays.

Imagination lives on memory:
That's true of love and war and thus of sport:
The world we love's a world that used to be.
Its sprinting figures cannot now be caught
But break the flashlit tape perpetually,
Though all their life's a yellowing report.
Forgive me, then, if speaking of what's next,
I make the past a presence in my text.

For me it starts in 1956,
The Test against the Indians at Lords
As Roy runs in to bowl and Hutton flicks
A long hop to the crowded boundary-boards.
Or did he miss? Or hammer it for six?
But I don't care what *Wisden*'s truth records.
When I dream back, the point is not the facts
But life enlarged by these imagined acts.

Forgive, then, the large licence I assume:
What I know's not the truth but what I like.
The Matthews final found me in the womb
But still I went to Wembley on my bike.
When Zola Budd sent Decker to her doom
The gods had aimed their wishes down the pike.
This isn't just a question of my bias:
All members of my tribe are bloody liars.

2 The Origins of Sport from Remote Times

Listen now, how far back sports began,
With cavemen at the weekends throwing rocks.
To play, it seems, is natural to man
(On rainy days they sat comparing cocks)
And woman too: the Amazons of Thrace
Could score far more than *one hundred and eighty*.
Their arrows wipe the smirk off Bristow's face
And Jocky Wilson's. *Mugs away then, matey*.
The Greeks wrote rules to make sport orthodox;
Found purposes – to keep the *mens* quite *sana*,
To stop Achilles going off his box
On finding he could not be top banana.
It was the smart alternative to war,
Although the two were closely interlinked,
As when at times they added up the score
And half the opposition were extinct.
If sport can blend the savage with the best
It illustrates a human paradox:
Meanwhile we're hoping for a classic Test
And, for our friends Australia, a pox.

3 The Olympics

As schoolkids know, the modern games began
In 1896 with Coubertin,
A count who thought sport must be amateur.
At this the Ancient Greeks would all demur:
O'Sullivans and Gunnells and Bulmerkas
Far out-earned the nymphs and vineyard workers;
Sponsored by the cities they were from
The Baileys and the Johnsons earned a bomb.
Their Linford had his lunchbox cast in gold
(Of which a million replicas were sold,
For though their names were never on the cup
It helped mere mortals keep their peckers up).
They'd tell you where to stick your laurel leaves.
All this the modern punter quite believes,
For human nature, magnetized to greed,
Is eager to disguise excess as need.
And since the winnings tended to be heavy
(Back before the Horse Race Betting Levy)
Then as now there was unsporting rancour:
Ancient Greeks yelled *Oi ref you're a wanker*
As loudly as the crew down Cold Blow Lane –
As wild, as leonine and as insane.
Surprisingly, the Spartans won the prize
For good behaviour, though this could be lies:
More likely, when they saw they could not win
They kicked the opposition's chariots in.
A Christian emperor banned it as a cult
Because his team could not get a result.

On grim estates at dawn, on college tracks,
In rings, in wheelchairs, velodromes and pools,
While we snore on towards our heart attacks,
They will outstrip the bullet and the fax,
They will rewrite the body and its rules.

Athletes who amazed Zeus and Apollo,
Rivalling their supernatural ease,
Must make do nowadays with us, who follow,
Breathless, on a billion TVs.
Should we believe it's us they aim to please?

The purpose stays essentially the same:
To do what's difficult because they can,
To sign in gold an ordinary name
Across the air from Georgia to Japan,
To change the world by mastering a game.

The rest of us, left waiting at the start,
Still celebrate, as those the gods adore
Today stake everybody's claims for more
By showing life itself becoming art,
Applauded by a planetary roar –

The gun, the clock, the lens, all testify
That those who win take liberties with time:
The sprinter's bow, the vaulter's farewell climb,
The swimmer who escapes her wake, deny
What all the gods insist on, that we die.

4 Football! Football! Football!

My sporting life (may I refer to me?)
Was never all it was supposed to be.
Mine was a case of talent unfulfilled.
I blame society, which blames my build.

From trap and pass and backheel in the yard
To deskbound middle age is something hard
For the Eusebio of '64
To grasp: you don't play football any more.

Your boots and kit are all gone into dust,
And your electric pace a shade of rust.
Whatever knocks the football fates inflict
On Shearer now, your chance of being picked

If England reach the Mondiale in France
(Does Umbro really make that size of pants?)
Is smaller than the risk of being brained
By frozen urine falling from a plane,

And though you'll stop by any rainy park
To watch folks kick a ball until it's dark,
You don't expect Dalglish will seek you out
To ask you what the game is all about.

But more fool him, you secretly suspect:
You've seen the lot, from Crewe to Anderlecht,
From Gornik to Stranraer to River Plate,
The Cosmos and Montrose and Grampus Eight,

The Accies, Bochum, Galatasaray,
Finbogdottir, Dukla Prague (away),
Botafogo, Bury, Reggiana . . .
Football! Football! Football! Work? *Mañana*.

Sponsored by IKEA and by Andrex,
Butch in sacks or mincing on in Spandex,
The great, the mediocre, the pathetic,
Real Madrid and Raggy-Arse Athletic–

Twelve quid a week or fifty grand an hour,
The game retains the undiminished power
To stop the clock, accelerate the blood
And sort the decent geezer from the crud.

From 5-3-2 to Kaiser Franz libero
Is there a team formation you don't know?
Experience! There is no substitute
When working out why Andy Cole can't shoot.

The fields of dream and nightmare where the great
Line up beside the donkeys to debate
Who gets the league, the cup, the bird, the chop
And whether Coventry deserve the drop

Are graveyards of a century's desire
To keep the youth that sets the world on fire –
Pele's '58, Diego's '86,
And Puskas hushing Wembley with his tricks . . .

And back, and back, to James and Meredith
And all the tricky Welsh who took the pith,
Until West Auckland marmalize Juventus –
World on world through which the game has sent us,

Until at last we stand in some back lane.
You're Cantona but I'll be Best again.
Who gives a toss what any of it means
While there are Platinis and Dixie Deans?

There life is always Saturday, from three
Till *Sports Report*, as it's supposed to be,
The terrace in its shroud of freezing breath,
Hot leg, crap ref, a soft goal at the death,

Fags and Bovril, bus home, bacon sandwich –
Paradise in anybody's language
Is listening for the fate of Stenhousmuir
(Robbed by Brechin 27–4).

5 Amerika

The subtleties are wasted on the Yanks.
They like their football players built like tanks.
And find it hard to understand that skill
May well produce a scoreline of nil–nil.

A journalist in Minneapolis
Enquired, 'Hey, what kind of crap is this?'
The Majors' baseball strike had cancelled out
What all his summer columns were about.

And he'd been sent to watch Bulgaria's
Brilliant but nefarious
Stoichkov–Lechkov–Kostadinov team
Punch holes in half of football's so-called cream –

Although this fact had somehow passed him by.
It seemed to his uneducated eye
This game was kind of complicated, weird
And somehow even longer than he'd feared.

'This thing', he said, 'has possibilities.
But let me tell you how it really is.
America means *short attention span*,
So let me run some changes past you, man.

'We want a wider goal, a bigger ball.
We want real bricks in the defensive wall.
We want the pitch divided into four
Plus fifteen time-outs making room for more

'Commercials. That, my friend's what we call sport.'
Poor sod, one more imagination bought
And rented out to commerce as a site
Where money = nation = right.

It seemed from watching the Atlanta Games
Americans alone possess their names;
That those who came to represent elsewhere
Might just as well not bother being there.

Of course this wasn't a deliberate act,
But it revealed a national want of tact.
America exists to be the best:
And second's nowhere; second's for the rest.

But I remembered, while the strike was on,
How this friend's friend and I had one day gone
To watch a minor league game in the sticks –
A bunch of has-beens taking on the hicks.

That summer's end between two railroad yards
Were men whose lives were faded baseball cards,
Who wound it up and from their far-gone youth
Unleashed in dreams the balls that baffled Ruth,

Or hammered one past Nolan Ryan's ears –
The kind of thing a failure stands and cheers:
When all you are's a mortgage and a job
You'd like to kick the crap from Tyrus Cobb

Or pass Ted Williams' average by a street.
This is your other life, the short and sweet: –
The afternoon when you're DiMaggio
And some girl wants to meet you, called Monroe . . .

All that was just a trick played by the light,
But since then, if I have a sleepless night
I listen for the sound of far-off trains
Like those that carried teams across the plains –

To me they sound like poems in the air
By those who write their epics then and there:
An hour's enough for immortality,
And if they had to they'd still play for free.

Noonday

The sultry back lane smells of fruit and shit
While everybody's binbags wait, stacked up
Like corpses in the ditch before Byzantium,
Late morning on the last day in the world.
The sun stands in the heavens. One by one
The binbags split asunder to disgorge
White regiments of maggots seething quietly.
At Rhodes, the Knights concealed the engineer
Who fashioned them the leather stethoscope
That diagnosed the sappers in the walls;
But gave the Sultan's nephew back to death –
And what is there in this to understand?

Great Suleyman, the one men call Magnificent,
Let it be night. Now let us hear the owl
Calling in the towers of Afrasiab,
The spider spin in ixarette around the Porte
The caravels go home to Venice burning
And in a velvet bag the severed head
Be brought for your inspection. No reply.
So later, from the noonday heat, we come
To beg the shade and silence of an hour
In Suleyman's branch library at Rhodes,
A cool white cage five paces cross, where nothing
Dares to live or rot without his word.

Lines on Mr Porter's Birthday

Nowadays
People are worried by art-historical poems,
Made angry by musico-literary-critical poems,
And pissed off by serpentine dream-driven poems
With Audenesque spoilers and Browningesque trim.
Some are driven to spasms of spittle-flecked rage
By poems with bits of Italian or German left in,
And made to feel
Anxious and sweaty and dim
By poems regarding the past and the future as if they were real.
Nowadays 'people' say,
Porter? Oh, Porter, we cannot be doing with him.
He's too hard. It's elitist. It's not of this age.
When readers are ignorant, cowed and ashamed,
Appearing on film as a stammering blur
Which (due to a forthcoming court case) regrettably cannot be
    named,
When popular culture comes on like the Stasi
And the last decent mag is away down the khazi,
When it's all up with us, and the sky has gone black
And the gods will not, repeat not, no, never be back,
When all the above preconditions occur
And about the whole compass stretch oceans of shite,
When the sun has just offered the moon the third light
You may fairly suppose his prognosis was right.
Yet here in the meantime the poems of Porter
Enliven the cortex and flush the aorta,
Make wine-of-aesthetics from Westminster water.
The world may be doomed but the bugger can write.

Postcards to the Rain God

for Peter Didsbury on his fiftieth birthday

1

Pluvius shelters under the hawthorn
At the end of Reservoir Lane
In an old gaberdine and a cricket cap,
Listening intently
For that handful-of-thrown-gravel sound.
The hills have all vanished. Excellent, excellent.

2

With echoes drowning
In far-below darkness and silver,
Wedged on the slippery ladder
In rags in the stinking brick shaft
With his newspaper turning to papier mâché,
He drinks the drips
That fall from the manhole cover.

3

She stands for a moment in the florist's window
When lightning and downpour
Have emptied the lunch-hour street
And the sky has gone purple.
She looks out through a bouquet of wet bloody roses
She holds in a kid-gloved hand, smiling
At her own perfume, feeling wet silk on her skin
And biting her rose-coloured underlip.

4

The house has been up for sale for months.
An old legal family down to its uppers,
Haunting the rotten, trapdoored passageways,
Drowned in the mirror
The brother, the sisters, doolally, then dead,
With an orange tree bursting the greenhouse.
Sad, very sad, intones the locality, watching.
You can't see him but he's there:
The after-downpour smell of shit and dockleaves
From the blindside of the fence.

5

The narrow brick foot-tunnel under the railway
Smells of rain and bonfires
And something else that might be sex.
Some of the oldest leaves in Northumberland
Lie there for the diversion of the rambler.

6

The bank on the corner of our street
Wears its impractical lead-cladded helmet
In honour of archers
Who practised in fourteenth-century rain
With blistered string-fingers
And anvils of cloud overhead.

7

When you are in the swimming bath
And it rains on the glass roof so loudly
You can hear above the swimmers' cries,
It is pornography.

8

Damp gravels on the landscaped bombsites
Where a long-term experiment (long enough
to see the life cycle of the Packamac)
Studies the transformation of asbestos prefabs (1947)
Into adipose and cancer. Rain doesn't help.
But think of the concrete made utile!
The slab-roads laid down as for Shermans and Churchills
Along the old drainsites –
Miles of straight and dry white lines
Up which the rain advances
Between the sheds of the allotments,
Gauzily, roaring.

9

To take ship.
The White Ship (not that one)
Clearing the mouth of the Hull,
The rebel banner raised
At the arsenal. Rain like grape-shot
Scalding the canvas. Below decks
Prince and poet, drinking Bastard,
Bowed to his diary of rain.

10

The field is much bigger than when you arrived.
The old gas, the old rain,
Have come up from the ground towards teatime.
A Craven 'A' drizzle to greet them.
The girls have gone indoors
An hour ago in their ill-advised late-summer
Cottons and heels. Like peasants
You carry the posts home.
Split boot and wet arse,
And a shite-coloured dog to go with you.

11

You sit in your shed in the rain.
In its peppercorn racket
You have a much better idea:
Marks on paper, made from the pluvial sexual
Ink of the Iris and Pearson Park pond-rain.
Messages unread, a century
From now: *Today a cloudburst settling*
Its anvil on the slates,
Then longer, softer rain – I cannot tell you how –
Is like piano-islands
In the pond. Ad
Maiorem Pluvii gloriam.

Synopsis

In the small, the final, town of X,
If you should feel about to leave
The Home Guard will remove your brains.

You'll hear them turning up
With ladders and a stirrup-pump
Beneath your windows, pissed and shushing.

Next day you'll feel as if there's water
Trapped in your ears and walk dazedly round,
Tilting your head like the Persons of Mad

Who litter the place in a surplus of Heritage,
Taking you back to its ancient foundation
By lepers and saints, 'by the one river twice'.

Passing the doctor in the market square
You see him nod approvingly,
Brandishing a bag of crabs you might suppose

Extracted from the pubic hair of corpses.
You're bidden to dinner that evening.
God's in his Heaven, so he cannot help.

In spring you'll wed the doctor's daughter,
An asexual vampire type of a girl
With coathanger bones and one enormous

Middle tooth, which in another life
You might suppose was joking. As things stand
Your nights will all be ecstasy instead.

You will give up your job as a poet
To work in her dress hire shop –
Ballgowns for Walpurgisnacht,

Glass slippers, ropes of hair;
And in your evenings as a potman mutter
Cryptic, hopeless warnings to the next

Poor sod whose train has left him here
As it left you, although you won't remember.
If you're lucky he might read you this.

Ex Historia Geordisma
a sorrowful conspectus

I *from* THE GO-AS-YOU-PLEASE SONGBOOK

'*Tha divvent sweat much for a fat lass, hinny*'
ST CUTHBERT THE SPOT-WELDER

'*Lyric poetry is not possible after Darlington*'
MURDO (YOUR CHIEF STEWARD THIS MORNING)

The A66 in Cumbria was blocked for several hours today by early
medieval warfare.

The reason for the collapse of Germany in 1945, said Geoffroi,
fingering his Hornby coal-tender, was the diversion of so many
troops to assist with the removal and transport from galleries
and palaces, east or west, of gold, art treasures *et cetera*. Hence
also the congestion of the railways. *Mint!*

The holly; the ash; the bale-fire; the birch; the stony scriptorium;
the critics; the stotties; prayer-frost and repentance; bring
back the birch, for the sons of birches. *I'm with you now*, said
Biffa. Canny.

A FRUIT

'*Jesmondo! Mondo Jesmondo!*'
EL CANTO JESMONDO

Hand me that banana now.
The great big blue one on the shelf.

Behind the scrim
And the cinnabar yoni

And the hostas. Look,
Look. Are you blind? Over *there*.

Give me that blue banana now
That I may ease myself

And think of entire
Historical periods.

You do not – *hélas* –
You do not understand.

You, a mere man,
How can you grasp the banana,

You who do not like it up you,
Eh?

Winter again with the forces of Northern reaction,
Vanguard of the 'bitter' ampersand,
The marmoreal slash.
The Modernist incontinence!
Pale scolds with posh addresses,
Still more Socialist than you, like.
The little presses fold away like trousers,
Dead men's trousers with the hanged
Tongues sticking out. *For in my Father's house*
Are many trousers. All shall be
Donated to await the gratitude.
Let a filing cabinet be named for this
And launched at Monkwearmouth
At nightfall with torches.
The corpse of the erstwhile promoter
Delays in the mouth of the Tyne
That underlined remark that changes everything,
L'esprit d'escalier submarine.
Shall these bones live? – Not
If we can help it, Sonny. Not round here.

Poem for a Psychiatric Conference

'Thou thyself art the subject of my discourse.'
BURTON, PREFACE TO *The Anatomy of Melancholy*

'Melancholy is . . . the character of mortality.'
BURTON, 'The First Partition'

I

When Marsyas the satyr played and lost
Against the god Apollo on the pipes,
The god lacked magnanimity. He skinned
The howling creature to his bones and tripes,
There in the nightmare canvas by Lorraine
Arcadia is green, and deaf to pain.

II

You were staring, one teatime, into the sink
When the voice made its awful suggestion. It seems
You were really, or ought to be, somebody else
In a different house, with a different wife –
May I speak plainly? the voice enquired.
It glozed, like the serpent in Milton –
Turned out for *years* you'd been making it up:
The kitchen, for one thing, the tiles and the draining-board,
Drawing-pinned postcards and lists of to-do's,
Even the crap round the back of the freezer.
The evidence *after all spoke for itself.*
The view up the steps to the garden, for instance,

The lawn with its slow-worm, the ruinous glasshouse
Up at the top, where the hurricane left it half-standing.
The woman next door as she pinned out her washing.
The weathercock's golden irregular wink
In the breeze from the sea to its twin on the spire
A mile off. Besides, the grey Channel itself
Setting out for the end of the world
Was the wrong stretch of water beside the wrong town.
You stood with your hands in your pockets and waited.
Very well, then, the God in the details disclosed:
Bus-tickets, receipts, phone numbers of people
You shouldn't have met in the pub
At the wrong time of day, the wrong year
With the wrong block of sunlight to stand
In the doorway. Your tread on the stair-carpet:
Wrong. Your skin between the freezing sheets
At dusk: an error. No matter the cause.
There is error, but not correspondingly cause.

III

The name of your case is *depression*
Although Doctor Birmingham favours
A failure of nerve. The files on the desk
In his office are fifty years old
And he, it seems, is just pretending
That he works here, sharing your gloom
And your startled glance out at the slice
Of bitter-green grass where a bottle
Keeps rolling about in the wind
At the top of the city, where everything –
Buildings, the streetmap, the people –
Has run out of steam and delivered the ground

To an evil Victorian madhouse
Complete with cupola and coalhole
Which may or may not have shut down,
Though the bus shelter waits at the gate.
The overcooked smell is like weeping,
The cries are like nursery food
And the liverish paint on the wailing walls
Is a blatant incitement to stop being good.
Call for Nurse Bromsgrove and Sir Stafford
Wolverhampton, call Rugeley the Porter.
There are vast misunderstandings
Lurking in the syntax by the stairs.
The worst of it is, there are rooms
Not far off, waiting and book-filled
For someone like you to arrive and possess them;
A hedge at the window, and lilacs, and past them
A street that can take a whole morning
To saunter downhill past the flint walls and ginnels
Adding up to harmless privacy. This perhaps
Is what some of the mad people contemplate,
Reading their hands on a bench in the park
In their ill-fitting clothes, as if someone must come
To explain and restore and say *Put that behind you.*

The Railway Sleeper

We are entering *L'Angleterre profonde*, which does not exist. We apologize for any delay and for the inconvenience history may have caused to your journey. On leaving the train please ensure you are completely possessed.

1

This was a siding or maybe even the entrance to a spur. Coal wagons rested here for weeks during winter strikes or in the overnight panic when the Luftwaffe breached the main inbound line. You could look it up. There are archives and historical maps.

Somewhere a ceramic map is mounted on a lost brick wall which is no longer understood to be part of a station. It has been part of a school, a bookshop, a restaurant, and now it is nothing especially and looks out on nothing. It is not part of its own map: the remembered smoke goes by on the other side of the hill, in the next valley, in different livery, its passengers eating different pies and drinking different brands of beer. A mad old bloke is seeking out such facts even as this sentence forms: what he needs next is an audience, this man you may become.

2

White sky of a summer evening. A green light waits at the entrance. No one up at Fat Control has bothered to switch it off. Meanwhile the roadbed vanishes slowly under willowherb, dock, the moraine of mud and grit sliding back into the cutting. The metaphysics of material culture.

3

The old come here to walk their dogs, the young to fuck each other, the middle-aged to fuck their dogs. It is a sex landscape, the far edge of legitimacy, the last ditch where fences turn to paper, boundaries waver and goats are secretly housed among the hawthorn scrub. A site of penetration, excretion and unrecognizable objects, or of objects inexplicably deformed, such as a briefcase full of concrete. What a story that could tell! if its mouth were not full of concrete. This is a branch of railway land, cousin to the sunset pang as the lines divide at York, or the much-abridged viaducts of Leeds, or the vast white elephant of Liverpool Edge Hill – that sexual warehouse and carpark.

4

The train and its landscape, you must understand, is a sex. An iron sex, an oil sex, a coal sex, weed-dripping-bottom-of-the-sandstone-cutting sex, the red-raw backbroken sex of exhausted navvies and their whores, and the choked sex of collapsed embankments, earthworks of the 1840s. This is the sex of modernity: lost to us now; the language and the gestures of blood, iron, crusty upholstery, leather window-straps, and twelve-inch toppers full of concrete.

5

The Omar Pound. The Elaine Jackson. The Cushie Butterfield. The Grave Maurice. The Trial to His Family. The Bring Me the Head of Dr Beeching. These are some possible names, possibly archived by the aforementioned head-the-ball for the great steam revival when we step back in tight formation, following the railwaymen's silver band, down the cutting into the smoke of the nineteenth century under light rifle fire from the tribesmen. We are retching, lousy and spavined by rickets, but strangely happy, listening later at the tunnel's mouth for oracles of rich disaster.

6

I am lying in bed when the train goes by – on summer nights, that blue sound, like remembering an unlived life. And another, and another, audible here at the triangle's centre. Promises, promises. The fulfilment of desire on the chilly evening sands of far-off resorts where the fathers parade with their shirt collars flattened on their lapels and the mothers say it's getting on Ted and you suppose it is, though you're not Ted. You're you, just listening. Cacophonous plumbing awaits you. The sexual creak. The fart of unbuttoned self-regard. The sound of waves, of trains; the silence of the blue night that frames them.

7

Nobody knows what desire is: a train brings you to the threshold with a suitcase and your sister, with your preoccupied parents. Desire is a street opening for the first time as you walk: gasholder, graveyard, pie-shop, cobbler's, church, the ribbed fishermen's terraces climbing back into black and green woods. *Thalassa! Thalassa! Railways! Railways!*

8

No one knows what desire is. It is here and not here. Running
down the steps to the beach as the tide pulls back under fog you
feel belated. A train is crossing the long bridge over the narrow
neck of the bay. The curtains of the great hotel are drawn, its
alpine gardens shrivelled with salt.

9

A man with rusty hands has strained for fifty years to shift the
points. In his back pocket waits a piece of paper with a word
written on it in dried-blood copperplate: *homoerotic*. Neither of
you would know what it meant. Around him the ashy fields
of sidings are afire after sunset. Yonder lies Ferrybridge, lies
Castleford. He bends like a reaper to his task. He serves the sea
by sweating there so far inland after the sea trains have gone.

10

A woman draws the curtains, turns from the window and leaves
the room but comes back to peer out again at the line that runs
at the end of the garden. It is a long evening in late summer, the
heavy blueness hanging everywhere, and visible among the
branches the one green eye.

11

It may be that I lie upstairs, unsleeping at this very moment, sent
to bed at summer's end, in the last thick light, *A la Recherche*
Volume One abandoned on the counterpane in favour of this
English reverie, so intimate that England seems abroad. The
smell of heat and rot beneath mown grass. A frog on the garden

path. A creosoted shed settles minutely towards the ruin it will meet long after its owner's death. And round its head-high hand-carpentered shelves wait box upon box of locos, tenders, carriages and waggons; cardboard boxes, their angles and edges worn down to reveal the gingery weave of their stiff cardboard; boxes driven out to the end of the garden by a female disapproval that despises things for merely being things, or details, or imitations of serious objects.

12

Wrexham. Gentlemen. Do Not Cross the Line. Kein Trinkwasser. Penalty Forty Shillings: Byelaws of the Railway: these letters in cast-iron relief, brick-red on range-black, stolen themselves along with their supporting post and borne away (but how? on a crossbar? by barge up the silty, corpse-rich canals which are the ghost-twin Abels to the Cain of rail?) to a backyard in Thirsk, a growing collection of rail-realia in Coalville, a car-park in Hinckley, a salt-rotted lean-to in Millom. Our barmy old party is writing everything down, amanuensis to an abolished god with wings of fire, a surveyor's telescope and a black top hat. Railway flora: scorched dock and desiccated willowherb; crisp groundsel for Billy the budgie.

13

In the tallest heaven, a frost of summer stars. Below, black branches against blue air. The train is coming but I have to sleep. The mouth of the sleeper silently opens. There is the faintest breath like the suspicion of a train entering the far end of a long tunnel, one of those Pennine epic glitter-black inner spaces, consecrated to the drip of *Urmutterfurcht*.
There is nothing to be afraid of yet.

The Genre: A Travesty of Justice

for Jo Shapcott

'The Porter found the weapon and the glove,
But only our despair can find the creed.'
DEMETRIOS CAPETANAKIS, 'Detective Story'

CHAPTER ONE

Do we live in small murderous towns
Where history has ended up?
Under their grubby insignia,
Summed up by mottoes
In greengrocer Latin? Do we reside
In the abolished Thridding? Have we always?

Were our towns constructed
From coal or manure, as kaufmanndorf
Or jakes, at a trivial confluence,
By deadly caprice (*oh let it be he-ere*)?
Divined in scripture? Destined
To defeat the understanding?

Are ours the homicidal sticks
In whose early spring evenings
Armies of policemen go down on their knees
In the scrub by the taken-up sidings?
Or do they peer from the edge of gravel pits
At frogmen who shake their slow heads,

Pointing like embarrassed Grendels
To a larder paved with torsos?
Do we answer these questions
Without taking legal instruction?
Can we not see how the trap is left
Open to claim us, the blatant device,

The traditional fit-up? Can we
Be what the atlas has in mind,
Twelve miles from a regional centre
With adequate links to the coast
And a history of gloving and needles
And animal products?

Is this the back of our station,
The clogging stink of the tannery yard,
And are these our gnats in suspension
Above the canal, and this our melancholy
Born of contiguity and quiet,
Whose poets are not very good?

Is this the poet? The immense
And anxious-making egg of his head?
His vast squirearchical torso?
His air of always being somewhere
Else in spirit as he turns
To hold your gaze a moment

And discard it? Is the poet
Here tending his irony, making a phrase
With the same offhand stylishness
Seen when he's chalking his cue
Or admiring the sheen of his waistcoat
In the smoke-filled mirror

In the afternoon hall, unfussily
Clearing the colours? And are those
His friends the police, who salute
With their pints, and not for the first time
Declare he's too clever by half?
Is this the poet? Well, is it?

CHAPTER TWO

These are towns you might hear about
Once, on a regional station
While driving home late in midweek, sweaty
And scared from committing adultery, Trevor.
I see you remember it now.
Towns where a chemical lorry
Has entered the lives of a greengrocer's family
Via the front room bay window
(Somewhere preserved, through the first
Million aeons, for grandparents' corpses).
Just think, if you'd thought, you'd have known
That the place would be everywhere next
On account of the murders, but you?
Well, Trevor, you were just too busy shagging.
Your honour, I must now refer to those
Small bitter towns at the heart of the fifties
Where unmarried daughters are nursing their parents
To death, and then snatching an hour
With Margery Allingham, Dorothy Sayers, Miss Silver,
Inspector Alleyn, and perhaps, with a flush
Half discontent half disgust, Miss Blandish.
See them, the fortyish daughters of Albion,
Put on their sensible shoes,
Their conscientious hats, their commendable gloves

And set out on their level-headed bikes
(Unknown to themselves, in formation)
To do good in their towns of curmudgeons.
Nuneaton, Hinckley, Ferrybridge, Drax –
The spinsters go cycling religiously
Out past fields of cooling towers
(They lend one another perspective),
Cross by the footbridge on clackety here-I-am heels
Between trains, in the railways' enforceable hush,
And enter the laurel-and-shadow-stuffed grounds
Of the hospital. Each may reflect that
When I was a girl . . . When I was a girl
The entire damned place was exactly the same.
And on they go with brave self-loathing past that Nissen hut
Unaware of the occupants strapped to their beds,
Who will die of a leak from the place in the woods.
And still our ladies love
Their awful town, its canal full of cats,
And its vicar, his knob in the mangle.

CHAPTER THREE

Arrowsmith, Bettshanger, Condon, Devine,
Evinrude, Fimister, Golightly, Heathcote,
Isbister, Jupp, Kingsogmore, Lobb-Leppard,
Motherwell, Nethercott, Orpington, Poad,
Quinnsworth, Ranfurly, Spaven, Terhune,
Urfe, Vandervelde, Woosnam, Younghusband
And Zimmer, who says he was framed.

*

They are not what they seem, my old cocker,
These names in a book, in a file
Or incised in old gold

On the greeny-grooved obelisk
Marking the dead of two wars
Where on market days madmen foregather

To issue their joint declarations,
Urgently letting us know
We should shove it right back where the sun don't shine.

Beside them the market goes on selling buckets
And James Hadley Chases and Jansons and Cheyneys
And knicker elastic and tripe.

They are not what they seem –
Lives of the lant-makers, lens-grinders, bailiffs
Arrested mid-gesture, their heads shot away

In every war since Sidney got his death,
The wind blowing through them
Like cats to be put out at night.

These are the people who stretch on the landing and groan
And go on with the business of living,
The murdering-murderee classes of England

Found rubbing the sleep from their eyes
Or indifferently turning a page of the *Argus*,
For what with one thing and another

They must have five minutes
To think about nothing or sex
Or an ivy-grown gateway they never did

Get through as children, yon side
Of the churchyard whose slim barrel-tombs
Are not mentioned in Pevsner. No,
Not what they seem, not at all, old cocker my lad.

*

Alison Arrowsmith, dead in a ditch,
Walked out with a soldier, came back in a box.
– It's the men says her mother, the men,
Obeying imperatives straight from their cocks.

– It's the times, says her father, half cut at noon,
And somebody's just got to do something soon.
He was last noticed resting his brow in the Gents
While the town got a handle on recent events.

Up at the paper, hot-metal sweat,
There isn't a clue or a suspect yet,
So the Friday edition is short of a page
And the editor's deep in an alky-red rage.

CHAPTER FOUR

Clocks, clocks, what about clocks?
What about all those station clocks
Ticking away like tyranny prophesied
In waiting rooms where stolid old benches
Spend for ever trying not to fart
And the ghosts of governesses wait
To be apprised, abused, sent
Packing with never a penny? Tick.
Afternoons. Seasons. Epochs. Tick,
A railway age in Bradshaw's hell.
Cold spring sunshine. The random

Brambly lash of the March rain. Tick.
The immortal half-length clocks,
Complacent moustachioed minor gods
Of the up-line, the down-line,
The sinister spur to the quarry,
The girls' school, the old place
The army had out in the woods. Tick.
When you are dead the clocks will step out
On the platforms and wink at each other
Before you go by, with your throats cut,
One per compartment, blood smeared
On the strap of the window, the photo of Filey,
Your faces, your crusty good coats, the matching
Crimson carriage cloth. Stiletto heels of blood
Tick away down the corridors. These trains
Are special. Tick. Their schedule is secret,
Their platform remote from the roar
Of the great vaulted terminus. Tick. They are coming
To get you one dim afternoon
With a John Dickson Carr in your bag
And a packet of three, or a cake for your auntie.

CHAPTER FIVE

I am the one you've been looking for,
The singular first person
Here at the death.
        The square-ended shout
Has gone up from the stand,
So the Duchess's Cup has raced
Into the records again
In a thunder of wall-eyed no-hopers
And foul-mouthed effeminate midgets in silk,

While round at the back of it all, in the sheds,
Among mowers and oildrums, down on my knees
In a doorway of sunlit Victorian dust,
I done it. I mean, I done *this* one.
I lie in my caravan, feeling it rock
On its bricks by the abattoir. Windy.
I'm scanning *Reveille* for creatures like me,
The bad apples of Lustgarten's eye,
From the class that has feeble excuses and onanists' tremors,
The work-shy, enthralled by America,
Reached by race-music picked up at the fair
With the clap and the ravenous
Oil-based charm that makes us at home
Among engines in pieces and under the skirts
Of your daughters. Our sort are barbers
And butchers gone bad
From a failure of deference.
I do hope you're writing this down
And ignoring my fraudulent idioms.
They look for a soldier. They fancy a Yank
Off the airbase. So let them.
Come rain on the roof, come wind,
I lie here and rock. I'm awful. I've sinned.

To Be Continued

Notes on 'The Underwater Songbook'

Songs from the Drowned Book was written as part of *The Book of the North*, a project devised by W. N. Herbert, in which poets, novelists and visual artists collaborated in an alternative history of the North. *Songs from the Drowned Book*, including poems by W. N. Herbert and Katrina Porteous, was subsequently set to music by Keith Morris and performed at Newcastle BigFest in July 1999. *Songs from The Black Path* forms part of a film script in which I supplied the verse material and Julia Darling wrote the story in prose. *Songs from Downriver* is part of a jazz musical written in collaboration with the composer Keith Morris.